D1288965

7/09

J954
B

FOCUS ON
India

ALI BROWNLIE BOJANG and NICOLA BARBER

WORLD ALMANAC® LIBRARY

Please visit our web site at: www.garethstevens.com
For a free color catalog describing World Almanac® Library's list of high-quality books
and multimedia programs, call 1-800-542-2595 (USA) or 1-800-387-3178 (Canada).
Gareth Stevens Publishing's fax: (877) 542-2596.

Library of Congress Cataloging-in-Publication Data

Brownlie Bojang, Ali, 1949-
    Focus on India / by Ali Brownlie Bojang and Nicola Barber.
        p. cm. — (World in focus)
    Includes bibliographical references and index.
    ISBN-10: 0-8368-6721-1   ISBN-13: 978-0-8368-6721-3 (lib. bdg.)
    ISBN-10: 0-8368-6728-9   ISBN-13: 978-0-8368-6728-2 (softcover)
    1. India—Juvenile literature. I. Barber, Nicola. II. Title. III. World in focus
(Milwaukee, Wis.)
    DS407.B73   2006
    954—dc22   2006001923

This U.S. edition first published in 2007 by
World Almanac® Library
An Imprint of Gareth Stevens Publishing
1 Reader's Digest Rd.
Pleasantville, NY 10570-7000 USA

This U.S. edition copyright © 2007 by World Almanac® Library. Original edition copyright ©
2006 by Hodder Wayland. First published in 2006 by Wayland, an imprint of Hachette Children's
Books, 338 Euston Road, London NW1 3BH, U.K.

Commissioning editor: Victoria Brooker
Editor: Nicola Barber
Inside design: Chris Halls, www.mindseyedesign.co.uk
Cover design: Wayland
Series concept and project management by EASI-Educational Resourcing (info@easi-er.co.uk)
Statistical research: Anna Bowden
Maps and graphs: Martin Darlison, Encompass Graphics

World Almanac® Library editor: Gini Holland
World Almanac® Library cover design: Scott M. Krall

Picture acknowledgements.
The author and publisher would like to thank the following for allowing their pictures to be
reproduced in this publication: Chris Fairclough Worldwide/ Chris Fairclough 4, 31, 40, 41, 42, 53,
57, 58, 59; Corbis 5 (top) (David Samuel Robbins), 8 (Paul Almasy), 9 (Reuters/Fayaz Kabali), 10
(Stapleton Collection/ Duncan Smith), 11 (Bettmann), 12 (Reuters/ Kamal Kishore), 13 (Bettman),
16 (Reuters/ Punit Paranjpe), 18 (Lindsay Hebberd), cover, 19 (Eye Ubiquitous/ David Cumming),
22 (Reuters/ Sunil Malhotra), 23 (Reuters/ Fayaz Kabali), 24 (Reuters/ B Mathur), 25 (Reuters/ B
Mathur), 27 Reuters/ Kamal Kishore, 28 (Pallava Bagla), 35 (Reuters/ Stringer Image), 36 (Reuters/
Amit Bhargava), 37 (Reuters/ Jagadeesh Nv), 44 (Reuters/ Ramin Talaie), 45 (Jeffrey L. Rotman), 47
(Gian Berto Vanni/Corbis), 48 (Reuters/ Raj Patidar), 49 (left) (Michael Freeman/Corbis), 49
(right) (Reuters/ Sucheta Das), 54 (Gallo Images/ Martin Harvey), 55 (Jeremy Horner); EASI-
Images Rob Bowden title page, 5 (bottom), 6, 14, 15 (Miguel Hunt), 17, 20, 21, 26, 29, 30, 32, 33
(top and bottom), 34, 38, 39, 43, 46, 50, 51, 52, 56.

The directional arrow portrayed on the map on page 7 provides only an approximation of north.
The data used to produce the graphics and data panels in this title were the latest available at the
time of production.

Printed in China

2 3 4 5 6 7 8 9 10 09 08

CONTENTS

Cover: A Hindu wedding ceremony involving fifteen different rituals is performed in Bangalore.

Title page: Rajasthani women wear traditional dress at the Pushkar Festival, Rajasthan.

CHAPTER 1

India— An Overview

Modern India is a large and exciting country full of contrasts. It has magnificent buildings, such as the massive Agra Fort, and grim, crowded urban slums. Alongside its prosperous middle class, large numbers of India's population live in great poverty. It is a country that prides itself on a tradition of peaceful coexistence between people of different communities, but it has suffered violent religious clashes between Hindus and Muslims. At over one billion, its population is second in size only to China's, but, with a faster growth rate, India's population is set to overtake China's by the year 2030.

India has a long and rich history marked by invasions and occupations. It has experienced times of great wealth and prosperity and has been the birthplace of advancements in philosophical thinking and science. This tradition of working with new ideas continues today in the emerging and vibrant software industry that is helping to drive India's thriving economy.

▼ Agra Fort, in Uttar Pradesh, was built during the reign of the Mogul emperor Akbar as a fortress, and partially converted into a palace by his grandson Shah Jahan (reigned 1628–1658).

▲ An Indian woman shops for clothing at an outdoor stall in Varanasi, Uttar Pradesh.

India is a country with abundant natural resources, particularly coal and fertile land, and it is rapidly emerging as a major economic and political power. Its rate of economic growth exceeds that of most other countries, except China, and is faster than the United Kingdom, other European countries, and the United States. Yet, while economic prosperity has benefited a large and expanding middle class, this group of people represents only a minority of the population. India still displays a huge contrast between affluent, urbanized Indians and the millions of people who strive to make ends meet on a daily basis. Poverty, particularly in the countryside, remains widespread. In many cities, slums provide a startling contrast to slick, new, high-rise office buildings and hotels. Despite its booming economy, India still ranks as one of the world's poorest nations.

Many practices and traditions that have been carried out for centuries continue to this day,
particularly in the countryside. For example, subsistence farming continues largely unchanged and farmers still use oxen to plow the land. In many places, however, these small farms sit alongside modern farms that use the latest technology to grow scientifically produced, hybrid varieties of crops such as cotton, rice, and wheat.

The legacy of India's colonial history under the British is still apparent in its parliamentary system—India is the world's largest democracy—its judicial system, and in the use of the English language in commerce, business, and politics. Another legacy of its colonial history is the ongoing conflict, created in 1947 when India gained its independence from Britain, between India and Pakistan over the disputed northern territory of Kashmir. This conflict has brought the two nations to war and, more recently, to the brink of all-out nuclear war.

▲ Many Indians live in extreme poverty. These basic shelters are home to recently arrived families in Mumbai.

◀ India is at the forefront of the computer software industry, yet oxen are still used to plow farmland across much of the country. India is full of such contrasts between the old and the new.

Culturally and historically, India is very rich. It is the birthplace of two important world religions—Hinduism and Buddhism. The caste system, whereby a person's place in society is determined at birth, is still widespread in India although it goes against the Indian constitution, which bans discrimination. Despite the fact that India is made up of groups of people from different ethnic backgrounds and different religions, speaking many different languages, Indians have lived side by side over thousands of years and have a strong sense of belonging to one nation.

Physical geography

- Land:1,147,949 sq miles/ 2,973,190 sq km
- Water:121,390 sq miles/ 314,400 sq km
- Total area:1,269,338 sq miles/ 3,287,590 sq km
- World rank (by area): 7
- Land boundaries: 8,758 miles/14,103 km
- Border countries: Bangladesh, Bhutan, Myanmar (Burma), China, Nepal, Pakistan
- Coastline: 4,347 miles/7,000 km
- Highest point: Kanchenjunga (28,209 feet/8,598 m)
- Lowest point: Indian Ocean (0 feet/0 m)

Source: CIA World Factbook

 Did you know?

India is named after the Indus River. Today, the region through which the river mainly runs is Pakistan, but it was previously part of India.

▶ The wheel on India's flag represents the Dharma Chakra, a Buddhist symbol dating back to 200 B.C. The saffron, or orange-yellow, color stands for courage, sacrifice, and the spirit of renunciation; the white for purity and truth; the green for faith and fertility. Saffron is also associated with Hinduism and green with Islam, the two major religions in India.

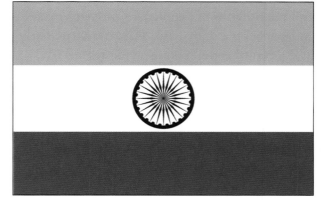

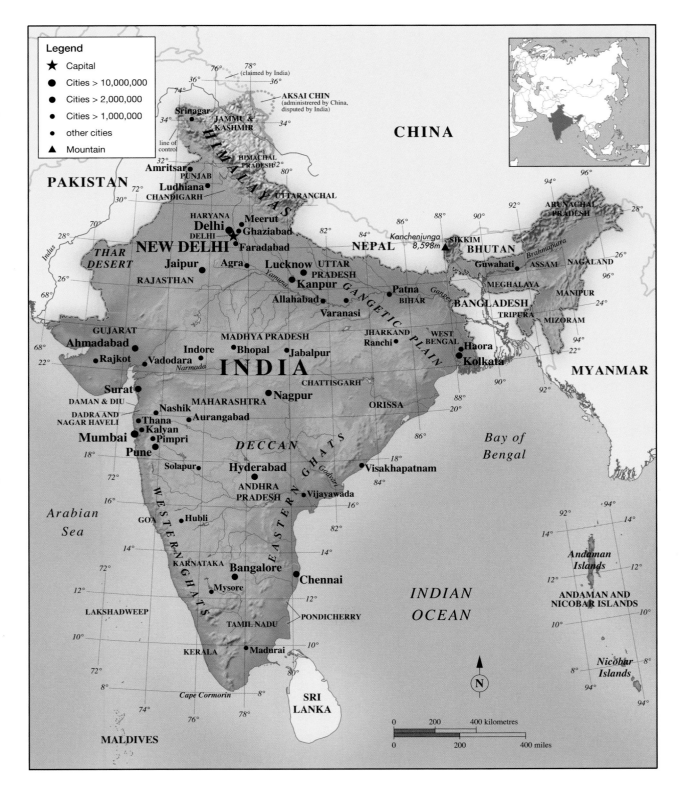

Legend

★ Capital
● Cities > 10,000,000
● Cities > 2,000,000
● Cities > 1,000,000
• other cities
▲ Mountain

76°   78°
(claimed by India)
36°   36°
74°   36°
AKSAI CHIN
(administrered by China,
disputed by India)

CHINA

Srinagar
JAMMU &
KASHMIR
34°   34°
line of
control
32°
HIMACHAL
PRADESH 32°
Amritsar
PUNJAB   80°
UTTARANCHAL

PAKISTAN   72°
Ludhiana
CHANDIGARH
30°
70°
HARYANA
Delhi   Meerut
DELHI   Ghaziabad
28°   **NEW DELHI** Faradabad
82°   84°   86°   88°   90°
ARUNACHAL
PRADESH   28°
THAR
DESERT   Jaipur   Agra   Lucknow   UTTAR   NEPAL   Kanchenjunga SIKKIM
                          PRADESH   8,598m ▲ BHUTAN
94°   96°
92°
26°
RAJASTHAN   Kanpur   Guwahati ASSAM   NAGALAND
68°   26°   Allahabad   Patna   MEGHALAYA   96°
Yamuna   BIHAR   Ganges   MANIPUR
Varanasi   BANGLADESH   TRIPERA   24°
                                                          MIZORAM
GUJARAT   MADHYA PRADESH   JHARKAND   WEST
68°   Ahmadabad   Ranchi   BENGAL   Haora   94°
22°   Rajkot Vadodara Indore Bhopal Jabalpur   Kolkata 22°
Narmada   **MYANMAR**
INDIA   CHATTISGARH
Surat   90°
DAMAN & DIU   Nagpur
DADRA AND   Nashik MAHARASHTRA   88°
NAGAR HAVELI   Thana Aurangabad   ORISSA   20°
Kalyan   86°
Mumbai Pimpri   DECCAN
Pune   Bay of
18°   Bengal
Solapur Hyderabad   18°
72°   ANDHRA   Visakhapatnam 84°
16°   PRADESH   Vijayawada
GOA Hubli   16°
Arabian   82°
Sea   WESTERN GHATS EASTERN GHATS Godavari
14°
72°   KARNATAKA Bangalore   14°
12°   Mysore   Chennai   **INDIAN
LAKSHADWEEP   OCEAN**
TAMIL NADU   PONDICHERRY
72°   10°
KERALA Madurai
8°   80°
74°   76°   78°   10°
Cape Cormorin 8°   **SRI
                                LANKA**
MALDIVES

92°   94°
14°   14°
14°
Andaman
Islands   12°
12°
ANDAMAN AND
NICOBAR ISLANDS
10°   10°

Nicobar
Islands   8°
8°
94°
94°

N

0   200   400 kilometres
0   200   400 miles

CHAPTER 2

History

India has one of the oldest and richest civilizations in the world, dating back over 5,000 years. For much of its history, the area we know today as India was made up of many different kingdoms and states. At times, these small states were united by dominant groups to create powerful empires, such as the Mauryan, Gupta, and Mogul empires.

THE INDUS CIVILIZATION

The earliest, large-scale settlements in India's history started around 3500 B.C. in the fertile valley of the Indus River in the northwest—an area that is now part of modern-day Pakistan. The civilization of the Indus Valley people was based on agriculture and trade. The main urban centers were Harappa and Mohenjo-Daro, and, like other large towns built by the Indus Valley people, they were carefully planned with broad streets and sophisticated systems for water supply and drainage.

From inscriptions found on clay tablets in the Indus valley, archaeologists know that the people of the Indus civilization developed ways of counting and measuring and that they had a written language. The Indus Valley civilization reached its peak in about 2500 B.C. but began to decline around 1700 B.C., possibly because of natural disasters such as earthquakes and flooding.

 Did you know?

At its height, the Indus civilization extended over .5 million sq miles (1.25 million sq km) across the Indus River valley and far beyond— as far south as Mumbai, as far east as Delhi, as far west as the Iranian border, and as far north as the Himalayas.

▼ The ruins of Mohenjo-Daro mark what was once the largest city of the Indus Valley civilization.

◀ A Buddhist monk prays at a monastery in Leh, which lies high in the mountains in the northern Indian state of Jammu and Kashmir.

HINDUISM AND BUDDHISM

From around 1500 B.C., the Aryans, a group of people from central Asia, began to invade India. As they moved south, they established control over much of northern India, building their capital at Delhi. Their arrival pushed most of the local inhabitants, known as Dravidians, into southern India. The Aryans had their own language, Sanskrit, in which they wrote their religious texts, known as the *Vedas*. These texts are the holy books for the Hindu religion which developed and took a strong hold throughout India. In the 500s B.C., another religion, Buddhism, was founded in India by a man called Siddhartha Gautama. He became known as the Buddha, "the enlightened one."

THE MAURYAN AND GUPTA EMPIRES

Other invaders into India included the Persians (from what is now Iran), who arrived in 530 B.C., and the Greeks, under the leadership of Alexander the Great, in 326 B.C. In 321 B.C., a local ruler called Chandragupta Maurya took advantage of the instability caused by the Greek attacks to found an empire which, during the reign of his grandson Asoka (272–232 B.C.), covered much of modern-day India.

During his reign, Asoka converted to Buddhism and encouraged the spread of this religion across his vast empire. After his death, the Mauryan Empire declined and fragmented. It was not until the rise of the Hindu Gupta dynasty in the A.D. 300s, founded by Chandragupta I, that the various kingdoms and states of much of India came together once again. The Gupta Empire, which lasted until about A.D. 500, was a time of great advances in both the arts and the sciences. Highly sophisticated Indian classical music and dance developed, and Gupta mathematicians invented both the decimal system and the Hindu-Arabic numerals that the West and international scientific community continue to use today.

THE MOGUL EMPIRE

The first Muslim invaders into India were Arabs who arrived as early as the A.D. 700s. They were followed by successive waves of invaders from Central Asia, including the Afghans and the Turks. The Muslim conquest of India began in earnest in 1192, when Muslim armies conquered much of northern India and established an empire known as the Delhi Sultanate. The Sultanate went into decline after the sack of Delhi by the ferocious Mongol leader, Timur, in 1398. A descendant of Timur, Babur, founded the Mogul Empire in 1526—a great Muslim empire that, at its peak under Emperor Akbar (reigned 1556-1605), covered almost the whole subcontinent. The Mogul Empire eventually crumbled at the beginning of the eighteenth century after a series of internal revolts. It was the British, however, who finally deposed the last Mogul emperor in 1858.

EUROPEANS IN INDIA

From the late 1400s, merchants and traders from Portugal sailed to Goa on India's west coast to trade for spices such as black pepper, cinnamon, and cloves. During the 1600s, British, Dutch, and, later, French traders challenged the Portuguese for this rich spice trade. With the permission of the Mogul emperors, the British East India Company set up various trading posts in India. During the eighteenth century, French traders became very successful in India, but after a series of battles between the two European powers, Britain emerged victorious. In order to protect its interests, Britain had entered into numerous agreements with local rulers and, gradually, its commercial interests became more political. The British East India Company expanded its power across much of India until the uprising of 1857, when Indian soldiers resisted with a year-long rebellion against British control. After this, in 1858, the British government took over the administration of the colony, and, in 1877, Queen Victoria was proclaimed Empress of India.

◄ This exquisite miniature painting comes from the *Akbarnama*, a history of Mogul emperor Akbar's reign that was written during his lifetime (in Arabic script, shown here). It shows Akbar on a tiger hunt.

THE MOVEMENT FOR SELF-RULE

Indian resistance to British rule led a group of well-educated Indians to found the Indian National Congress Party in 1885, and as the twentieth century dawned, India's movements for self-rule increased. During World War I, more than one million Indian soldiers fought in the British army. After the war, most Indians expected an increase in self-rule in return.

Instead, in 1919, British troops opened fire on a protest meeting in Amritsar, killing more than four hundred people. In the aftermath of this massacre, and to support the independence movement, Indian leader Mahatma Gandhi started his campaign of nonviolent disobedience against the British colonizers. He encouraged Indians to boycott British goods and to disobey laws that were considered to be discriminatory. As a way to control the colony, the British had long exploited the tensions between Hindus and Muslims in India, and the struggle for independence only increased these tensions. Muslims feared a Hindu-dominated government because the majority of India's population is Hindu. These tensions often erupted in extreme forms of violence as Muslims and Hindus alike blew up trains and carried out massacres against each other.

Focus on: Mohandas Karamchand Gandhi (1869–1948)

Mohandas Karamchand Gandhi studied law in Britain before living in South Africa, where he fought for the rights of Indian workers. He returned to India in 1914, where he became known as Mahatma, "Great Soul." He always advocated using nonviolence and passive resistance as ways of achieving political goals. One of the most famous examples of his methods was the Salt March of 1930. Salt was a basic necessity for everyone, but the British government both controlled the production and taxed the sale of salt. To draw attention to this, Gandhi and his followers walked 150 miles (240 km) to the coast, where they gathered lumps of natural salt—an illegal act under the British law. The British were unsure about how to deal with Gandhi, and often imprisoned him and his followers.

▲ Mahatma Gandhi (*left*) walks on his Salt March in 1930.

HISTORY'S BIGGEST MIGRATION

India finally won its independence on August 15, 1947. During the negotiations for independence, the Muslims, led by Mohammed Ali Jinnah, argued for a separate Islamic state. Despite the opposition of Gandhi, who believed that India should not be split up, increasing violence between Hindus and Muslims convinced the British viceroy (governor) of India, Lord Mountbatten, that dividing India into separate parts—termed Partition—was necessary. So the subcontinent was divided into the secular nation of India and the smaller Muslim nation of Pakistan, which was made up of two separate land areas on different sides of India. Then known as West Pakistan and East Pakistan, these two areas are now themselves two separate nations: Pakistan and Bangladesh. The plans for Partition were rushed through by the British, which caused millions of Muslims who were caught on the Indian side of the border and millions of Hindus, stranded on the Pakistani side of the border, to flee in opposite directions. Law and order completely broke down. In only a few weeks, an estimated one-half million people died, some through violence, others through the many hardships they encountered. In 1948, Gandhi was himself assassinated by a Hindu fanatic who believed that he was too tolerant of Muslims.

KASHMIR AND PAKISTAN

Jawaharlal Nehru, India's first Prime Minister, had a vision of socialist India and advocated government control of important industries. He drew up economic plans to boost India's agricultural and industrial output and adopted a policy of neutrality in foreign affairs. His rule was relatively peaceful, but he was succeeded by Lal Bahadur Shastri, who led two wars against Pakistan over Kashmir. The borders of this region in the north of the country had not been finalized at the time of Partition, and India and Pakistan have disputed the area ever since.

In 1971, the government of Pakistan sent forces into East Pakistan to suppress discontent over inequalities between the wealthier region in the west and the poorer, more isolated region in the east. The conflict between Pakistan and its distant eastern region sent millions of refugees into India from East Pakistan. India intervened and quickly defeated the Pakistani army. As a result of this war, East Pakistan broke away from Pakistan and became a separate Muslim nation, Bangladesh.

◀ Indian children dressed in the colors of the Indian national flag take part in a rehearsal for Independence Day celebrations in New Delhi, August 2004.

INDIRA GANDHI

After the death of Lal Bahadur Shastri, Nehru's daughter Indira Gandhi became prime minister (she was no relation of Mahatma Gandhi). During her two periods in office (1966–1977 and 1980–1984), there was considerable unrest. Her opponents objected to her dictatorial style of leadership, and indeed, she often abused her power by trying to suppress the media when they criticized her. When the opposition actually threatened her power, she called a state of emergency in 1975, and some 100,000 people were jailed without trial. In 1984, Indira Gandhi had to face confrontation with followers of the Sikh religion, who were demanding a separate Sikh state within India. When Sikh militants occupied the Golden Temple at Amritsar, a holy shrine for Sikhs, Gandhi sent in government troops. Several hundred people were killed and the shrine was badly damaged. As a direct result of this action, Gandhi was assassinated in October 1984 by two of her Sikh bodyguards.

ECONOMIC BOOM

In the early 1990s, India changed its political and economic policies. It followed the path taken earlier by China, opening up its markets to countries overseas and allowing private and foreign capital to be invested in the country. It built on its huge resource of well-educated but cheap labor to attract businesses to India. This strategy began the economic success that India is enjoying at the beginning of the twenty-first century. Tensions between Hindus and Muslims, however, have continued to trouble the country. The dispute between India and Pakistan over Kashmir has worsened, representing a major challenge for both countries in the future.

▼ Prime Minister Indira Gandhi addresses a crowd in New Delhi as part of her campaign for reelection in the general election of March 1971.

CHAPTER 3

Landscape and Climate

India claims an area of 1,269,338 sq miles (3,287,590 sq km), or slightly more than one-third of the size of the United States, although some of its area is disputed. It extends 2,000 miles (3,200 km) in length from the Himalayan Mountains in the north to its southern tip, where India is separated from the independent island country of Sri Lanka by the Palk Strait.

LANDSCAPE

India is often referred to as a "subcontinent" because it lies to the south of the great landmass of Central Asia and stretches out in a vast triangular peninsula. The Arabian Sea lies to India's west, the Bay of Bengal to its east, and the Indian Ocean wraps around its southern coasts. India is bounded to the north by the steep Himalayan Mountains.

The northern region includes the sandy, dry Thar Desert in the northwest and the huge expanse of the Gangetic Plain immediately to the south of the Himalayan Mountains, named for the Ganges River that flows through it. The Himalayas extend for 1,500 miles (2,400 km) along the northern and eastern borders of India.

? Did you know?

India occupies only 2.4 percent of the world's land area, but has approximately 15 percent of the world's population.

▼ Rajasthan, in the northwest of India, is known as the "desert state" because of its arid lands—including the Thar Desert. Camels are widely used for transporting goods in this region.

The second-highest mountain in the world, after Everest, is K2. Reaching 28,251 feet (8,611 m), it lies partly within India. The highest point completely within India, Kanchenjunga, at 28,208 feet (8,598 m), is also found in the Himalayan Mountains.

The Himalayan Mountains have been created by the collision of two of the plates that make up Earth's surface. This plate boundary is also the reason the region experiences earthquakes and landslides. The massive earthquake that hit the western state of Gujarat in 2001, for example, left more than 30,000

? Did you know?

K2 is so remote that it had no name until it was surveyed in 1856. The British surveyor, T.G. Montgomery, called it K2; "K" standing for Karakoram, the mountain range in which it lies, "2" meaning that it was the second peak he saw and listed. Today, K2 is the only major mountain in the world that is still known by the name given to it by its surveyor, rather than a common or local name.

people dead, and the earthquake in 2005 devastated much of Kashmir, killing about 75,000 and displacing about 3.5 million people.

South of the Gangetic Plain lies the immense, triangular Deccan Plateau. This high plateau extends to the southern tip of India at Cape Comorin. It is flanked by low mountain ranges called the Eastern and Western Ghats, with average heights of about 3,937 feet (1,200 m).

INDIA'S RIVERS

India is home to several large rivers, the most famous being the Ganges. Twenty-five percent of India's land area is included in its river basin. The Brahmaputra River in the far east has the greatest volume of water because it receives higher rainfall. Both these rivers rise in the Himalayan Mountains and carry rich, fertile alluvial soils to the Gangetic Plain, providing India with its most productive farmland and irrigating vast expanses of rice and cotton fields.

▼ Hindus consider the Ganges to be the holiest of all rivers. Each year, millions make their pilgrimages to the river at Varanasi to wash away their sins.

INDIA'S CLIMATE

Most of India has three seasons: a cool season from October to February, a hot season from March through to June, and then a wet season. In the south of the country, however, temperatures are more consistently warm or hot, even during the cool season, while the north has greater variation. For example, Chennai in the southeast has average temperatures that range from 75° F (24° C) in January to 90° F (32° C) in May and June. During the hottest months of the year, temperatures rise to extremes on the Gangetic Plain, sometimes going as high as 120° F (49° C).

In the mountain regions of the Himalayas, temperature is affected by altitude so that the average summer temperature is around 64° F (18° C) at 6,500 feet (2,000 m), dropping to 32° F (0° C) at 14,800 feet (4,500 m). Rainfall also varies across this huge country. In the arid Thar Desert in the northwest, there is virtually no rain, while the states in the far northeast receive over 390 inches (10,000 mm) of rainfall annually. Most of the country depends on the monsoon winds that bring rainfall to much of the subcontinent from June to October.

Focus on: The Indian Ocean Tsunami

On December 26, 2004, a tsunami hit the east and southwest coast of India and engulfed the Andaman and Nicobar Islands in the Bay of Bengal. The deadly tsunami waves were created by the most powerful earthquake in the world in forty years. The earthquake measured 9.0 on the Richter scale and rumbled beneath the sea just off the island of Sumatra in Indonesia. By the time the resulting waves hit the Indian coast, they were over 30 feet (up to 10 m) high and traveling at a speed of 18 mph (30 kph). In India, at least 10,749 people were killed, another 5,640 remain missing, and nearly 7,000 people were injured. The waves penetrated up to 1.8 miles (3 km) inland, destroying buildings and roads, harbors, and fishing boats in their wake.

◀ This aerial view, taken in January 2005, shows the devastation caused by the tsunami in Nagapattinam, a port 219 miles (350 km) south of the city of Madras.

THE MONSOONS

The monsoon winds are generated by the difference between air temperatures over the Asian landmass and the sea. From June to October, a southwest wind blows from the Arabian Sea and from the Bay of Bengal, bringing warm, moist air and heavy monsoon rainfall to much of India. For the rest of the year, a northeast wind blows dry air in from the landmass of Central Asia.

India is dependent on the monsoon rains. A late monsoon, or even an early one, can cause problems for both agriculture and the economy. Sometimes, heavy monsoons bring widespread and destructive flooding, such as the floods and landslides that hit Mumbai and the Maharashtra region in central India in 2005, killing over 1,000 people. In urban areas, many drainage and sewage systems cannot handle heavy rains and they frequently overflow, with dangerous and unhealthy consequences.

The monsoon rains decrease as the monsoon travels north, meaning that the northwest of the country is comparatively dry. Sometimes, however, the rains fail to extend their usual distance northward. In 2002, for example, the western state of Rajasthan was hit by severe drought when it received only about half of its usual rainfall. As their crops failed, thousands of people were forced from the countryside to look for work in towns such as Jaipur.

 Did you know?

The wettest place on earth is reported to be Mawsynram, in Meghalaya in the northeast of India. The average annual rainfall is nearly 470 inches (12,000 mm)—10 times more than New York and 20 times more than London.

▲ Umbrellas provide protection from the monsoon rains in Kerala state. The monsoon rains are a lifeline to India, but in some years they can also bring misery.

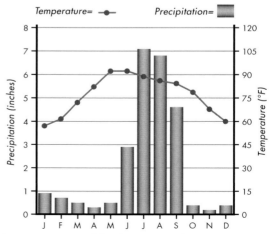

▲ Average monthly climate conditions in New Delhi

CHAPTER 4

Population and Settlements

India is the second country in the world after China to pass the 1 billion mark in population. Between 1960 and 2000, its population more than doubled from 442 million to 1 billion. By 2004, India's population was estimated to be 1,081,200,000. The size and rate of growth of its population puts a great strain on India's resources and its capacity to ensure the health and education of all its people.

ETHNIC GROUPS

The Indian population consists of two main ethnic groups. The Indo-Aryans make up 72 percent of the population and have their origins in the Aryan people who migrated into India about 3,500 years ago. The Dravidians form 25 percent of the population and live mainly in the south of the country. The rest of the population is made up of descendants of people who came from China and Mongolia, and tribal peoples known as Adivasis. India's population also includes very small number of British people and those of European origin whose families stayed in India after independence or who have settled there since.

POPULATION GROWTH

At the beginning of the twentieth century, the birth rate in India was high, but it was offset by an equally high death rate due to widespread diseases, epidemics, and famines. From around the middle of the century, however, the impact of improved health care, particularly mass immunizations, brought about a steady decline in the death rate. As a result, the rate of India's population growth soared.

In 1951, the government introduced family planning programs that promote the goal of having just two children per family to slow the rate of population growth. Education about

◀ A Toda couple wear traditional *poothukulis*, the Toda native dress. The Toda are considered to be one of the earliest (Dravidian) tribes of India.

population growth became part of the school curriculum, and birth control programs were run in hospitals and health centers throughout the country. In the mid-1970s, during the state of emergency, Prime Minister Indira Gandhi and her son Sanjay organized a highly controversial and unpopular program of forced sterilization for both men and women.

Although population growth has slowed down in India, many people still prefer to have a large family so that their children can contribute to the family income and care for their parents as they get older. In particular, boy babies are highly valued and many families continue to have babies until two sons are born. Many young women are married before the legal age of eighteen, and 49 percent of women give birth for the first time before they reach twenty. The government now recognizes the importance of more economic independence for women as one way of encouraging them to have fewer children, and it has policies in place to encourage girls to stay in school longer and marry later.

◀ As in this wedding in Bangalore, the Hindu wedding ceremony involves fifteen different rituals and takes about three hours.

Focus on: Gender Imbalance

Gender imbalance in India—the uneven ratio of girls to boys—is becoming greater. In 1981, there were 962 girls per 1,000 boys under the age of six. By 2001, there were 927 girls per 1,000 boys. Many Indian families prefer boy babies, and modern technology has enabled many parents to know the sex of their children at a very early stage of pregnancy, sometimes resulting in a pregnancy termination if the baby is a girl. Traditionally, boys are preferred for reasons of financial security: The male is seen as the main breadwinner and therefore more likely to be able to support parents in their old age. Another factor is that parents have to pay high dowries when the time comes for their daughters to be married, so boys may bring families less cost and more help.

DENSITY AND DISTRIBUTION

During the twentieth century, the average population density of India rose rapidly from 297 per sq mile (77 people per sq km) in 1901 to 826 per sq mile (319 per sq km) by 2004. Areas of high density are found not only in the heavily urbanized areas but also in intensively farmed rural areas, such as the fertile Gangetic Plain, where one- third of India's population lives. Some border areas also have high densities because of refugees coming into India from other countries, for example near Bangladesh, Myanmar, and Sri Lanka. The inaccessible, inhospitable mountainous regions of the Western and Eastern Ghats, the northeast, and the Himalayas remain less populated regions of India because of difficult living conditions there. These areas have population densities below 424 per sq mile (110 per sq km).

CITIES, TOWNS AND VILLAGES

India has some 2,500 cities with populations exceeding 20,000 people, but most of India's population—72 percent—lives in more than 500,000 villages. Nearly all large Indian cities have begun huge building programs and the United Nations predicts that by 2030, about 50 percent of India's population will be living in urban areas.

Population Data

- Population: 1,081.2 million
- Population 0–14 yrs: 32%
- Population 15–64 years: 63%
- Population 65+ yrs: 5%
- Population growth rate: 1.5%
- Population density: 851.78 per sq mile/ 328.87 per sq km
- Urban population: 28%
- Major cities: Kolkata 14,299,000; Mumbai 18,336,000; New Delhi 15,334,000

Source: United Nations and World Bank

◄ A growing middle class in India is creating a demand for modern apartment complexes, complete with shops, restaurants, banks, and schools. This development is in Mumbai.

► In India's cities, many of the poorest people live in makeshift slums, such as this one alongside the main commuter railway line into Mumbai.

Cities in southern and central India, such as Bangalore and Hyderabad, are growing very quickly as people move in from surrounding rural areas, looking to benefit from the growth of new industries such as information technology (IT). Parts of many Indian cities are now much like cities in the United States and Western Europe with shopping malls, office buildings, hotels, and restaurants. For the poor, however, life in the cities is often no better than in the villages. Across India, about 150 million people live in urban slums or on the streets, without adequate water supplies or waste disposal.

Village life is often in stark contrast to middle-class, urban life. Typically, villages are surrounded by fields that are farmed by the villagers. Amenities can be limited, perhaps just a small shop, a primary school, and a small temple or mosque. People work as farmers or carpenters, or make pots and pans, but as work becomes increasingly difficult to find, many villagers travel to local towns to look for alternative employment.

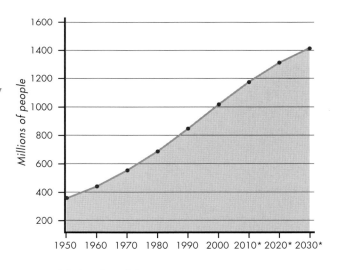

* Projected population

▲ Population growth 1950–2030

 Did you know?

The 28 percent of India's population who live in the cities are now equivalent to the entire population of India at the time of independence in 1947.

CHAPTER 5

Government and Politics

The violence that erupted between Hindus and Muslims after Partition has continued to trouble India since Independence in 1947. Both religious and regional differences have been the cause of serious outbreaks of unrest. For example, in 1992, widespread violence between Hindus and Muslims erupted after Hindu extremists demolished the Babri mosque at Ayodhya. A decade later, more blood was spilled in revenge when Muslims attacked a train carrying Hindu pilgrims returning from Ayodhya. Continued conflicts between Muslims and Hindus have sometimes severely threatened the democracy on which India prides itself.

Focus on: Ayodhya

Ayodhya, in the northern state of Uttar Pradesh, has been the focus of tension between Hindus and Muslims for many years. Many Hindus believe that it was the birthplace of Lord Rama, one of the main Hindu deities. In 1992, Hindu extremists demolished the sixteenth-century Babri mosque in Ayodhya, claiming that it stood on the site of a more ancient Hindu temple that marked the site of Rama's birth. Members of the Bharatiya Janata Party (BJP) were involved in the destruction of the mosque, and the BJP has since backed the construction of a Hindu Rama temple on the site. A makeshift temple has been constructed, but it remains a flash point for religious conflict between the two communities.

▶ Hindu extremists storm the Babri mosque in Ayodhya, December 1992.

INDIAN DEMOCRACY

India has the largest democracy in the world—it has more people voting in a general election than in any other country. During its general election of 2004, for example, about 660 million voters cast their ballots. In this election, India also became the first country in the world in which everyone voted by means of an electronic voting machine. Over one million machines were needed to cover the entire country.

Indian voters have plenty of political parties from which to choose—more than 500. The main national parties, however, are the Congress Party, which has predominated for most of the time since 1947, and the Bharatiya Janata Party (BJP), a Hindu nationalist party which promotes the concerns of Hindus in India. The BJP emerged as a major force in Indian politics in the 1990s. Its leader, Atal Bihari Vajpayee, became prime minister in 1998. In 2004, the Congress Party was voted back into power and Manmohan Singh, a follower of the Sikh religion, and a former governor of India's Central Bank, became prime minister. He is the first Sikh to become the country's leader.

◀ A Kashmiri woman enters her vote on an electronic voting machine in Sheeri, 40 miles (61 km) northwest of Srinigar, in the Indian general elections of 2004. Each party has its own symbol alongside its name. The BJP's symbol is a lotus flower; the symbol of the Congress Party is a hand.

NATIONAL AND STATE GOVERNMENT

India is a federal republic made up of twenty-eight states and seven union territories. The seat of Indian national government is in the capital, New Delhi. The president of India is chosen every five years by members of parliament, and is essentially a figurehead who represents India on ceremonial occasions. Real political power lies with the central government, which is based on the British system, with a prime minister and two houses of parliament—the upper Council of States (Rajya Sabha), and the House of the People (Lok Sabha). The Rajya Sabha has a maximum of 250 members, 12 of whom are selected by the president. The other 238 are elected by the parliaments of the twenty-eight states and seven union territories. In the Lok Sabha, up to a maximum of 550 members are directly elected by the Indian people in general

elections and two members can be appointed by the president. They serve for up to five years. The prime minister is advised by a council of ministers who are answerable to the Lok Sabha.

Each state has its own parliament, which is able to make specific laws for the state on matters such as health care, transportation, and education. The state governments are headed by a chief minister and the president also appoints a governor for each state. The national government, however, is able to impose direct rule from New Delhi if it feels it needs to, for example, during an emergency.

▼ The Indian Prime Minister, Manmohan Singh, at the European Union Business Summit in New Delhi, September 2005.

THE INDIAN CONSTITUTION

India is a secular state. This term means that the government officially remains separate from any one religion, allowing all forms of worship equal status. The Indian constitution is based on rights and democracy, and places a strong emphasis on ending inequalities in society and social welfare. For example, India's constitution requires the government to set goals for a minimum wage and subsidized health care. As a result of political corruption and the misuse of power, however, there have been times when the constitution has been ineffective in protecting the rights of Indian citizens. For example, during the Emergency in the 1970s, Prime Minister Indira Gandhi imprisoned those who opposed her and censored the press.

▼ Members of the Congress Party gather inside the central hall of the Indian parliament building in New Delhi to elect the head of their party in May 2004.

Focus on: The Gandhi Dynasty

The Nehru-Gandhi family has dominated Indian politics for most of its history since Independence. Indira Gandhi was the daughter of India's first prime minister, Jawaharlal Nehru. After her assassination in 1984, she was succeeded by her son Rajiv. He, too, was assassinated in 1991. His Italian-born widow, Sonia, was reluctantly drawn into politics to help the Congress Party win the general election in 2004. Although she declined the offer to become prime minister, Sonia took over the ceremonial role of party president. Her children, Rahul and Priyanka, both won seats in the 2004 election and appear ready to continue the Gandhi dynasty.

CHAPTER 6

Energy and Resources

Although stressed by the high density of its population, India is rich in natural resources, sources of energy, and farmland. Its rapid rate of industrialization and urbanization is creating a growing demand for energy to run new factories and supply businesses. The majority of the population still use traditional forms of energy, such as burning wood and dried cow dung for cooking and heating water, but increasing wealth creates demand for more energy to run appliances such as refrigerators and fans and, for the more affluent, televisions, washing machines, and personal computers.

India's energy consumption per person rose by about 44 percent between 1980 and 2000, compared to a 2 percent rise in the United States and 10 percent in the United Kingdom (UK) in the same period—one of the highest energy consumption growth rates in the world, along with that of China. Because of its relative lack of development compared to other countries, India's energy use per person is still only about 6 percent of the amount that people in the United States use, and 13 percent of that used in the UK. Pressure will increase as India's demand for energy grows at an expected annual rate of 4.6 percent up to the year 2010.

ENERGY PRODUCTION

Most of India's electricity is generated from burning coal, which it has in large reserves mainly in Madhya Pradesh, Bihar, and West Bengal. Experts estimate that these reserves, the fourth largest in the world after the United States, Russia, and China, will last until 2233. India also has reserves of oil and gas offshore from Mumbai, and in Assam and Gujarat.

◀ Energy consumption per person in India is low, but it is rising quickly as the demand for consumer electronics increases.

Another source of electricity of growing importance is energy from hydroelectric power (HEP). About 50 percent of HEP is produced by reservoirs high up in the Himalayas, while over 4,000 large dams have been built across major rivers elsewhere to provide plants that produce the rest. The increase in demand for energy for both industrial and domestic use has put pressure on India's energy sources —and has led to some controversial plans for supplying energy, such as the Narmada river dams.

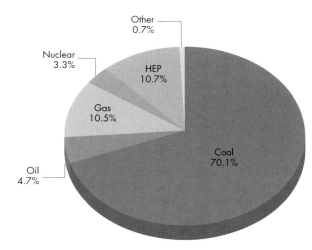

▲ Electricity production by type

Focus on: The Narmada Dams

The construction of large dams on the Narmada River has become one of the most important social issues in India, drawing world-wide attention. In 2000, as part of a major campaign against these dams, thousands of people marched and demonstrated to protest against the Indian government. The dams were built in spite of these protests, flooding the valley behind the largest of the dams, the Sardar Sarovar dam. This flooding deprived up to one million people, mostly poor farmers, of their homes and their land. In March 2005, the Supreme Court of India ruled that those who were displaced must receive fair compensation for their lands and homes.

▶ Demonstrators in New Delhi in November 2000 protest against the construction of the Sardar Sarovar dam.

Energy data

- Energy consumption as % of world total: 5%
- Energy consumption by sector (% of total):
  Industry: 27.1%
  Transportation: 12.3%
  Agriculture: 2.7%
  Services: 0.8%
  Residential: 55.6%
  Other: 1.5%
- CO_2 emissions as % of world total: 3.9%
- CO_2 emissions per person, in tons per year: 0.99
  Source: World Resources Institute

India has plans to increase the proportion of electricity that comes from nuclear energy—just 3.3 percent of power production in 2005—and has eight nuclear reactors under construction. India also has one the largest national programs in the world to promote the use of solar power. In many villages, solar power is not only more environmentally friendly than many other forms of producing electricity, it is more cost-effective as well.

MINERAL RESOURCES

In addition to its large reserves of coal, India's rich abundance of mineral resources includes iron ore, manganese, bauxite, diamonds, and limestone, as well as other valuable minerals.

India is one of the most important producers of iron ore in the world. Two-thirds of India's iron ore reserves are in the states of Orissa and Bihar. There is a global demand for iron ore to produce steel, especially from China. India also exports iron ore to Japan, Iran, and Taiwan. After Russia, India has the largest supply of manganese and other economically useful minerals such as bauxite and copper. Diamonds and other gems are also an important resource,

providing a valuable part of India's export industry. In Jaipur, Rajasthan, local gem stones supply a thriving jewelry industry.

LAND AND AGRICULTURE

Over half of India's land area is suitable for cultivation, providing a particularly valuable resource. Rice is the most widely grown crop, and it provides the staple food, cooked in a variety of ways, for 65 percent of the Indian population. The main rice-growing areas are in the south and the east. Rice is also cultivated on the fertile Gangetic Plain along with wheat, which is a staple food in northern India. The Deccan Plateau also has fertile black soils which are particularly good for growing cotton.

Indian cotton is the basis of the textile and clothing industry in India. Cotton accounts for 30 percent of India's agricultural gross domestic product. India's 4 million cotton farmers plant more land with cotton than anywhere else in the world and produce 12 percent of the world's cotton. Yields per acre are comparatively low,

▲ A worker picks cotton. These genetically modified plants are being field tested under controlled conditions in India.

however, so many farmers are interested in genetically modified strains of cotton that could improve yields. Some think this "gene revolution" could be India's new Green Revolution.

The world's largest tea producer, in 2005 India had nearly 40,000 tea estates employing a workforce of over two million. In recent years, however, India has faced increasing competition from Sri Lanka and Kenya as well as a general slump in global demand for tea. India is second only to Brazil in the production of sugar cane, and is the largest consumer of sugar in the world.

Woodlands cover 22 percent of India's land area. India's trees range from deciduous woodlands in its temperate northern districts to dense, tropical forests in its Western Ghats. Teak, rosewood, and sal are grown for furniture, while bamboo is used as scaffolding in the building industry. Although much wood is grown on renewable tree farms, deforestation is a major problem across the country.

Focus on: The "Green Revolution"

From 1967 to the late 1970s, the so-called "Green Revolution" changed India from an importer to an exporter of food. Following a number of failed monsoons in the 1960s, and its resulting dependency on the United States for food aid, India introduced new methods of agriculture to achieve self-sufficiency in food. The area of land used for agriculture was expanded, two crops a year were grown instead of one, and new strains of high-yield seeds, mainly wheat and rice, were introduced. The results were record grain crops in the late 1970s. The new methods, however, require increased use of fertilizers and pesticides, which can cause environmental problems. Improved irrigation led to dam construction, which also has a negative environmental impact.

▼ The current building boom in India creates an enormous demand for timber needed to build scaffolding and for framing concrete.

CHAPTER 7

Economy and Income

When it gained independence in 1947, India's economy was dominated by traditional agriculture and cash crops such as tea, sugar, and cotton. Now, its economy still includes traditional village farming, but commercial agriculture, handicrafts, modern industry, and a multitude of service industries—particularly information technology (IT)—play an increasingly dominant role.

ECONOMIC CHANGE

Before the 1990s, the Indian government exercised strict control over the economy, imposing high taxes on imports from abroad and limiting foreign involvement. This government control protected Indian industries and businesses from foreign competition, but, by the 1980s, it was clear that this system was stifling development, as Indian companies fell behind their international counterparts. From 1991, the government opened up the Indian economy to the outside world, allowing foreign investment, competition, and trade.

The government has set up free-trade zones, such as the Madras Export Processing Free Trade Zone, where foreign companies can invest without having to pay duties and taxes,

▲ Tea remains one of India's most important agricultural exports. This large estate in Kerala, southern India, is owned by Tata Tea.

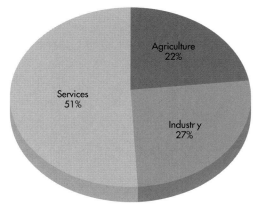

▲ Economy by sector

Agriculture 22%
Services 51%
Industry 27%

Economic data

- Gross National Income (GNI) in U.S.$: 674,580,000,000
- World rank by GNI: 11
- GNI per capita in U.S.$: 620
- World rank by GNI per capita: 159
- Economic growth: 8.6%

Source: World Bank

which makes it easier for manufacturing industries to develop. For example, sales of cars made in India increased between 2002 and 2003 by a huge 41 percent. In 2004, India was ranked among the top ten industrial nations with its gross domestic product (GDP) estimated to be worth over $2,200 billion and to be growing at a rate of more than 7 percent in that year.

INFORMATION TECHNOLOGY

A crucial factor in boosting India's economy has been its role as a front-runner in the fields of IT, biotechnology, and communications. In 1998, software and related IT services contributed about 1.2 percent to India's GDP. By 2004, this sector had grown to account for about 4.1 percent of GDP. This growth is expected to continue as increasing numbers of overseas companies move their software work "offshore" to India to benefit from India's low-cost engineers. Many companies in the UK and the United States have outsourced some parts of

their operations to India, particularly call centers, because they can pay Indian employees far less than they can pay workers in their home countries. There are over 40 software parks located around major cities such as Bangalore, Chennai, Mumbai, Puna, and Hyderabad.

AGRICULTURE

Despite all these changes in India's economy, agriculture remains an important factor in the country's economy. Sixty percent of India's workforce is employed in the agriculture sector, and agriculture still constitutes 22 percent of India's GDP.

 Did you know?

India is the world's third largest producer of satellites, and its INSAT system is one of the world's biggest domestic satellite communication systems.

▼ Women in a factory in Bangalore, Karnataka, wire circuit boards for TV production.

Focus on: Bangalore

The southern city of Bangalore, the capital of the state of Karnataka, was once known as a retreat for older people who were attracted by its temperate climate and relaxed atmosphere. By 2005, it was the fastest growing city in Asia and had become known as the "Silicon Valley of the East" because of its abundance of information technology jobs. In 2004, there were some 1,400 IT companies based in Bangalore, many of them foreign firms set up to take advantage of the city's vast pool of computer-literate, English-speaking workers. These companies have brought new prosperity to the city, employing over 160,000 people in the IT sector in 2005. IT employees are mostly young people who now have money to spend, and Bangalore's main shopping street, Mahatma Gandhi Road (or MG Road), is full of designer shops, restaurants, bars, and restaurants.

RISE IN CONSUMERISM

The booming Indian economy has created a powerful new group of people in Indian society, the so-called "middle class." This new middle class is thriving in both urban and rural areas and includes business people and wealthy farmers, professionals, and white-collar workers. They are well-educated and have disposable income to spend on leisure activities and goods such as fashion clothes and CD and DVD players. In turn, the increased purchasing power of the middle class helps boost the economy. In fact, India's own industries struggle to keep pace with people's demand for goods. This consumer demand means that India will have to import more goods unless it can increase the rate at which its manufacturing industries grow. Despite the growing prosperity of India's middle

▼ Modern shopping malls, such as this one in Jaipur, cater for a growing consumer class in India.

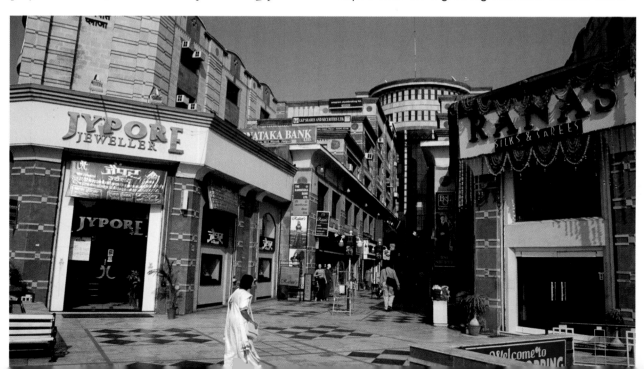

◀ A shoe-mender in a makeshift street-side store takes a break from his work. These simple stalls are typical of India's informal sector.

class, experts estimate that 35 percent of the Indian population continues to live on less than $1 a day, and 80 percent on less than $2 a day. India was ranked as low as 127 out of 177 countries on the United Nation's development index in 2002, which takes into account people's quality of life, including factors such as education and health, as well as their material wealth.

THE INFORMAL SECTOR

In some large cities such as Delhi, Chennai, and Mumbai, the economy's informal sector creates about 67 percent of total employment. The informal sector pays people who perform menial or temporary work, usually on a casual basis. These workers either never reach levels of income where they would pay tax, or they simply avoid paying tax altogether. Typical jobs in this sector include street vending, cleaning, working as security guards or domestic servants, and employment in textile workshops. Employment is frequently neither registered nor monitored and, as a result, the conditions in which people work are often unregulated, unhealthy, and dangerous. Many people who

work in this way are migrants from rural areas who have few skills and are therefore unable to get better-paid or more secure jobs.

▼ Every day thousands of items of laundry are processed here in the *dhobi ghats* in Mahalakshmi, Mumbai. This is an example of how India's seemingly chaotic informal economy can work smoothly.

CHAPTER 8

Global Connections

India has had strong trade links with the rest of the world for many centuries. In colonial times, many Indians went as indentured laborers to far-flung parts of the British Empire. They were promised fair wages and a trip home in return for a fixed number of years' labor. Some of these laborers chose to stay at the end of their indenture, and vibrant communities of people of Indian origin are now part of many parts of the world, for example, in South Africa and the Caribbean. In more recent times, India has experienced a "brain-drain" as many of its most educated people have moved to countries such as the United States. India's influence on music, art, cuisine, dance, religion, and science can be seen all over the world.

▼ Textiles of cotton and silk were some of the first goods to be traded by India. The textile industry is still an important part of India's economy. This factory is in Mumbai, India's main textile center.

INTERNATIONAL ORGANIZATIONS

India was a founding member of the United Nations (UN). Today, it works closely with the United Nations to achieve the Millennium Development Goals, a list of targets set by the UN to eradicate poverty, improve health and education, ensure sustainable development, and develop global partnerships by 2015. Like many other countries that were colonized by Britain, India has been an important member of the Commonwealth since its independence.

TRADE AND INVESTMENT

India recognizes the importance of links with other countries for its future prosperity, not only by means of trade but also by opening its doors to investment from other countries, and by itself investing in foreign companies. India's largest trading partner is the United States, from which it buys aircraft and parts, machinery, fertilizers, and computer hardware, among other goods. India's main exports are textiles and ready-made garments, agricultural products, gems and jewelry, leather products, and chemicals. Its other main trading partners are China, the UK, Belgium, Hong Kong, and Singapore. As a member of the World Trade Organization (WTO), India has had to reduce export restrictions and simplify its tariffs for countries importing their goods into India.

India is a leading member of two powerful country groupings, the G3 and the G20+. The G3, formed in 2003, is made up of Brazil, South

Africa, and India. Its purpose is to speak with one, powerful voice in negotiations with the rich, industrialized G8 countries (the United States, the UK, France, Germany, Japan, Italy, Canada, and Russia). The G20+ includes Argentina, Brazil, China, and South Africa, as well as India. This group of developing countries has built a common position to fight against the subsidies that are paid to farmers in the United States and the European Union (EU), and against barriers to agricultural trade. The G20+ has shown that it has a powerful voice. At a WTO meeting in Cancun, Mexico, in 2003, negotiators from G20+ pressed the EU and the United States to phase out of farm subsidies so that their own markets would not be flooded by inexpensive farm imports. The talks collapsed when the two sides could not come to an agreement. Negotiations have since continued with more success.

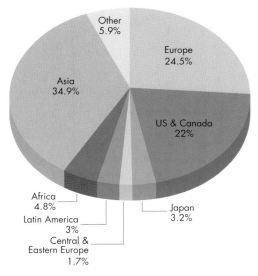

▲ Destination of exports by major trading region

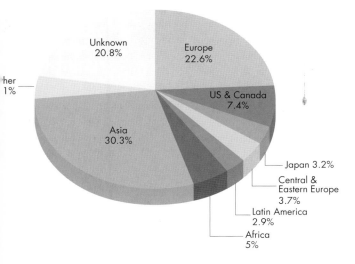

▲ Origin of imports by major trading region

▲ Indian soldiers guard the "line of control" in 2001 in the northern state of Jammu and Kashmir, near the disputed border with Pakistan.

RELATIONS WITH NEIGHBORS

Relations between India and its neighbor Pakistan have been strained since 1947. After Partition, disputes quickly broke out over the state of Jammu and Kashmir (often referred to simply as Kashmir) on the border of the two countries when the Hindu ruler of this predominantly Muslim state chose to become part of India. A UN cease-fire gave control of certain areas of Kashmir to each country. Neither side has accepted a divided Kashmir as a permanent solution, and two further wars have since raised a real threat of nuclear war. Both India and Pakistan have nuclear weapons and, in 1998, both countries carried out nuclear tests, partly as a way of intimidating each other. In 2004, the two countries agreed on a peace process over Kashmir, and hopeful signs emerged as India withdrew some of its troops and as bus services started across the disputed border region in Kashmir for the first time in sixty years. A rail link was opened between Pakistan and India, with a second one opening in 2006.

India has had disputes with its neighbors over water resources. In the 1960s, there were hostilities between India and Pakistan over India's construction of the Farakka Barrage on the Ganges River near the border between India and East Pakistan. The barrage, or dam, was completed in 1970, and diverts water out of the Ganges into the Bhagirati-Hoogly River. After its independence in 1971, Bangladesh continued to press the case against India, claiming that the dam deprived Bangladesh of vital water resources. Another dispute with Pakistan is over the construction by India of the Baglihar hydroelectric plant on the Indus River in Kashmir. The dam is due to be completed in 2007, and Pakistan has asked the World Bank to arbitrate between the two countries.

▶ Dr. Naresh Trehan works in an operating room in New Delhi. Dr. Trehan moved to the United States in 1969, where he was a highly successful heart surgeon. He has since returned to India, prompted largely by Indian nationals who were seeking his services in the United States and asking why they could not get the same quality of care back home.

India's relations with China slowly improved at the end of the twentieth century after many years of tensions over borders. India and China now share much in common as emerging, vibrant, Asian economies. In 2005, talks between the two countries focused on how they could cooperate to develop their own software technologies and other mutual interests.

WORKING OVERSEAS

Since the 1970s, migrant Indian workers have been going to work in oil-rich Saudi Arabia. By 2004, some three million Indians were working there. The money they send home is a vital source of income for many families, although some reports claim that many Indians in Saudi Arabia work in very poor conditions in hospitals, peoples' homes, and service industries such as garbage collection.

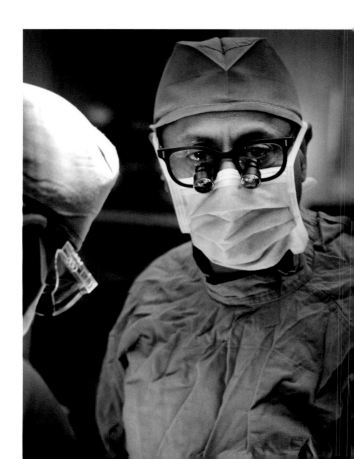

Many professional Indian men and women, particularly those working in IT and the professions, including doctors, nurses, and engineers, have been actively recruited by agencies in the United States and the UK. An estimated 1.6 million Indians are now concentrated in California, New York, New Jersey, Illinois, and Texas in the United States. According to World Bank figures, India receives more money than any other country from its migrant workers abroad—$17.4 billion in 2003.

Focus on: Call Centers

Many companies in the United States and the UK have outsourced work to call centers in India. These call centers handle a wide range of processing jobs, from answering customer service calls to telemarketing, credit demands, and accounting. Companies such as British Telecom have moved large parts of their operations to India to take advantage of lower wage costs. UK companies can make savings of an estimated 40 percent by outsourcing in this way. A good supply of well-educated and skilled workers in India is a major attraction for international companies. One prediction says that India will employ two million people as call center operators by 2008.

▼ An Indian woman answers a call at a call center in the southern Indian city of Bangalore.

CHAPTER 9

Transportation and Communications

A good transportation system is essential to the economic growth of any country and particularly one the size of India. Increased economic activity and development is putting pressure on the government to modernize and improve all of India's transportation networks.

? Did you know?

Indian Railways runs almost 14,000 trains, on 39,290 miles (63,230 km) of track covering 7,068 stations, and carries more than thirteen million passengers every day. With sixteen million employees, Indian Railways is the largest civilian employer in the world.

INDIA'S RAILWAY SYSTEM

The British began the construction of the Indian railway system in 1853, and within fifty years 23,000 miles (37,014 km) of track had been laid. The railways have expanded to become the most important mode of transportation for the movement of goods and people around India. Although the trains and train cars are often built to lower standards of comfort than in the West, trains are affordable

▼ People wait to wish departing relatives and friends farewell at a station. Trains are the most affordable means of long-distance travel for the majority of people in India.

and usually efficient. Drawbacks remain: Commuter trains taking people from the suburbs to work in city centers are often crowded, with many hanging on dangerously to the outside of the trains.

In order to ease its traffic chaos, Delhi opened a new metro system in 2003. The metro has a total length of 13.2 miles (21.3 km) of track and eighteen stations. Most of the track is elevated and the cars and stations are air-conditioned. The metro is integrated with other forms of transportation, such as bus and rail, to make travel as easy and efficient as possible. Mumbai has also been investing in improvements to its suburban railways that link its rapidly expanding suburbs to its city center.

ROAD TRANSPORTATION

India has the third-largest network of roads in the world, totalling 1,569,650 miles (2,525,989 km). Only slightly more than half of these roads are paved, however, and only 4 percent conform to internationally recognized standards. In many country areas, roads are no more than single lane paths that are impassable in heavy rains. The most important highway is the so-called Golden Quadrilateral, 3,633 miles (5,846 km) of road linking New Delhi, Mumbai, Chennai, and Kolkata. The government is upgrading 6,200 miles (10,000 km) of this road by 2012 at a cost of $6.9 billion. The World Bank is also investing $665 million in road projects around India, to do such things as improve rural roads in selected areas.

India is struggling with a staggering increase in its number of cars and other vehicles. Numbers have been doubling every seven years since 1970, and today about sixty million vehicles travel on India's roads. India is infamous for its cities' traffic jams, in which the streets are clogged with cars, motorbikes, and auto rickshaws—three-wheeled taxis with space for two passengers. In addition, the rapid increase in road traffic, poorly regulated licensing of drivers, and the poor state of the roads has led to high accident rates across the country.

► Rush-hour traffic in Jaipur is a chaotic mix of rickshaws, motorbikes, and a growing number of private cars. The same is true for other cities in India, causing major congestion and pollution problems.

AIR TRAVEL

India's vast size and the slowness of train travel make air travel an attractive option for those who can afford it. New budget airlines are mushrooming in India. The boom was started in 2003 by Air Deccan, based in Bangalore, when it offered fares between Delhi and Mumbai for a price as low as 500 rupees (U.S.$20/£11). Many airlines, such as Kingfisher Airlines, Spice Jet, and Go Air are following suit to provide cheap, no-frills alternatives to the major airlines.

GETTING CONNECTED

In the year 2005, India had an estimated 25 million Internet users. Up from some 5.5 million at the beginning of 2001, this is a huge and rapid increase, although still small in terms of the percentage of the total population. For the inhabitants of rural areas, getting connected to the Internet can present problems because electricity supplies are often intermittent (and in some places non-existent), and landlines for telephones often provide unreliable and slow links. New wireless technology is being piloted in some rural areas to explore alternative ways of connecting rural villages to the Internet.

Mobile phones were first introduced in India in 1994. At this time, only a few privileged people could afford to use them. Prices have fallen, and by 2003, it was estimated that, at around 25

▼ A young man logs onto the World Wide Web at an Internet café in New Delhi.

Focus on: High-speed Links

India is one of the first countries in the world to provide high-speed Internet access from trains. By 2004, some 24,900 miles (40,000 km) of fiber-optic cable had been laid around the country to provide communication links—not just for trains but also for cybercafés in train stations to serve local communities.

million users, India had more cell phones than fixed landline phones. At this time, India was adding an estimated two million cell phones every month and was the fastest growing telecommunications market in the world.

THE PRESS

During the Emergency, under Indira Gandhi, the government tried to prevent newspapers from writing articles that were critical of their policies. Today, however, the Indian press is independent, and lively debates take place over important issues of the day. India has more than 5,000 daily newspapers in many different languages.

▲ A newspaper and magazine stand displays a wide range of papers. Although Hindi is India's official language, English-language papers are the most widely read and include the *Times of India, The Hindu, The Statesman, The Indian Express,* and *India World.*

Transportation & Communications

- Total roads: 1,569,650 miles/2,525,989 km
- Total paved roads: 900,194 miles/ 1,448,655 km
- Total unpaved roads: 669,455 miles/ 1,077,334 km
- Total railways: 39,290 miles/63,230 km
- Major airports: 333
- Cars per 1,000 people: 6
- Mobile phones per 1,000 people: 25
- Personal computers per 1,000 people: 7
- Internet users per 1,000 people: 1

Source: World Bank and CIA World Factbook

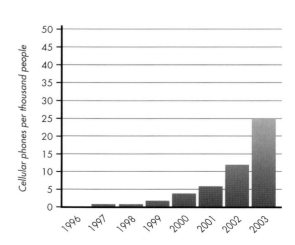

▲ Cellular phone use 1995–2003

CHAPTER 10

Education and Health

Since Independence, India has recognized the need for its people to be well-educated and healthy if the country is to develop and progress as a nation. With 35 percent of its population under the age of fifteen, India is faced with a huge task. Nevertheless, literacy rates have risen dramatically since Independence, from 15 percent in 1947 to 61.3 percent in 2002.

THE EDUCATION SYSTEM

Each state in India has its own system of education, so standards vary as some states invest more in education than others. For example, the state of Kerala at the south-western tip of India has prioritized education and has the highest literacy rate in the country, at 90 percent. Across the country, primary and middle school education from six to fourteen years is free and compulsory, although parents must buy books and other equipment for their children, which is a struggle for many poor families. Secondary or high school is not free,

and parents must pay fees for tuition as well as equipment. Private schools are popular among the upper and middle classes. Many secondary school students go on to higher education at university or college.

POOR-QUALITY EDUCATION

While all children should by law go to primary and middle school, in many states the record of attendance is poor. India has nearly 600,000 primary schools, but many of these are small village schools, often with dilapidated buildings and no facilities. A shortage of teachers hurts rural areas, and it is common for teachers not to show up for classes—on average, teachers in India are absent from the classroom for 25 percent of the time. The quality of the teaching is sometimes poor, and the curriculum being taught fails to capture the interest of many pupils. In 2004, about 135 million pupils were enrolled in primary and middle schools. Records kept from 1996–2003, however, show that only 80 percent of boys and 73 percent of girls actually attended school. The government is making great efforts to improve the quality of the curriculum that is taught in schools. The government is also encouraging participation at a local level, with Village Education Committees and parent-teacher associations that give parents more direct involvement in the education of their children.

◀ Boys at a private school in Delhi play soccer in their school's playing fields.

SECONDARY AND HIGHER EDUCATION

By secondary school, the number of students attending has dropped to 51 million (from 135 million), indicating that many children leave school early to work, or because their parents cannot afford to keep them there.

Many of those who succeed in secondary school go to one of India's 256 universities or 12,000 Institutes of Higher Education. Every year, India produces about three million graduates. India's education system has traditionally placed emphasis on mathematics and the sciences, resulting in a large number of science and engineering graduates.

▶ Lessons are held outside at this rural primary school in Rajasthan. Many schools in India lack proper buildings and equipment.

Focus on: The "Brain Drain"

Indian universities produce 135,000 engineering graduates each year. The most skilled are often tempted to move overseas for better pay. Despite the fact that salaries for those working in IT in India increased over 23 percent between 2001 and 2004, these salaries still represent only a quarter of their equivalents in the United States. Many people consider this "brain-drain" to be a huge loss of human capital and investment in education for India. Others claim that Indians learn new skills abroad and point to the large amount of money that is sent back to India by these workers. Some recent evidence indicates that the "brain-drain" is starting to slow down as Indian's economy continues to grow, and as the domestic job market becomes increasingly attractive to educated workers.

Education and Health Data

- ▭ Life expectancy at birth, male: 62.6
- ▭ Life expectancy at birth, female: 64.2
- ▭ Infant mortality rate per 1,000: 63
- ▭ Under five mortality rate per 1,000: 87
- ▭ Physicians per 1,000 people: 0.5
- ▭ Health expenditure as % of GDP: 6.1%
- ▭ Education expenditure as % of GDP: 4.1%
- ▭ Primary net enrollment: 77%
- ▭ Pupil-teacher ratio, primary: 40.7
- ▭ Adult literacy as % age 15+: 61.3%

Source: United Nations Agencies and World Bank

▲ An official checks the finger markings of a baby girl to make sure she has been immunized for polio.

DIFFERENCES IN HEALTH CARE

Standards of health care in India vary widely. In urban areas, large hospitals boast the latest medical technology for those who can afford to pay for treatment. In many rural areas, health care is poor, and many people live miles away from the nearest basic health facilities. Government health expenditure in 2002 was 6.1 percent of GDP, but over the years it has not grown to meet the increasing demands and needs of the expanding population.

Many poor people in India suffer from diseases that are a direct result of their living conditions. Malnutrition, poor sanitation, and lack of clean drinking water are the main problems, causing diseases such as typhoid and dysentery. Children who are weakened by malnutrition have little resistance to various diarrheal diseases, and these diseases are the main cause of childhood death. Although the infant mortality rate (the number of infants under age one dying per year) has fallen, it is still 63 per 1,000 children born—a high figure compared to the United States, where it is 7 per 1,000 births, or the UK where it is 6 per 1,000. By some measures, such as immunization rates, standards are actually falling. In 1994, for example, 91 percent of children were vaccinated against polio and 96 percent against tuberculosis; in 2002 these figures had dropped to 70 percent and 81 percent, respectively. Malaria, tuberculosis, and leprosy are prevalent throughout India.

As urban India adopts more Western life-styles, fast-food restaurants and more sedentary jobs are creating changes in the health of young Indians. Not surprisingly, these changes mainly affect the affluent upper and middle classes, and about 30 percent of India's well-off teenagers are estimated to be overweight. Changes in diet and the increase of obesity is causing concern about future health problems, particularly coronary diseases.

HIV/AIDS

The number of people with HIV/AIDS is steadily rising in India, and this disease poses a huge potential problem for the future. In 2003, the estimated number of people living with HIV/AIDS in India was more than five million, and between 20 and 25 million are predicted to be suffering from this disease by 2010. The spread of HIV/AIDS is attributed mainly to prostitution, the sexual habits of some migrant workers—particularly long-distance truck drivers—the use of unsterilized needles by drug addicts, and infected blood used for transfusions. Widespread ignorance and fear of the disease is being addressed by government programs that aim to educate people about HIV/AIDS and encourage young people to adopt safe and responsible lifestyles.

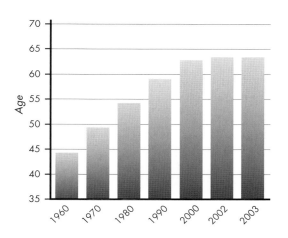

▲ Life expectancy at birth 1960–2003

Focus on: Medical Tourism

In 2004, George Marshall, a 73-year-old violin repairer from Bradford in the UK, paid $8,425 (£4,800) to have a heart bypass operation in a hospital in Bangalore. At home in the UK, he had been faced with the choice of waiting six months or paying about three times more for the operation. In the same year, 150,000 people visited India for treatment. By 2012, this kind of "medical tourism" is estimated to be worth 100 billion rupees ($2.1 billion/£1.24 billion) to India.

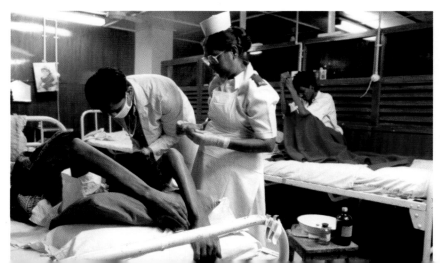

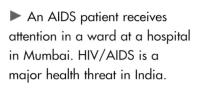

▶ An AIDS patient receives attention in a ward at a hospital in Mumbai. HIV/AIDS is a major health threat in India.

CHAPTER 11

Culture and Religion

With its historical mix of peoples from many different parts of Asia and Europe, and its population of more than one billion people, it is impossible to speak of any one single Indian culture. Strong cultural and historical threads, however, have helped develop a strong sense of nationhood among the Indian people.

LANGUAGES

Many different languages are spoken in India. The national language of India is Hindi, but it is the first language for only 30 percent of Indians, most of whom live in the north. The vast majority speak one of fourteen other official regional languages. Hindi is one of the family of Indo-European languages, and others in this group that are spoken in India include Bengali, Gujarati, Punjabi, and Urdu. People in the south of India speak Dravidian languages such as Kannada, Tamil, Telugu, and Malayalam. Most educated Indians speak several languages. English is India's second official language, commonly used for business, commerce, politics, and higher education.

 Did you know?

In addition to the official regional languages of India, more than 1,650 different dialects are also spoken.

FOOD

Not surprisingly in a country as large and diverse as India, food varies from region to region. It also varies according to culture and religion. For example, Hindus do not eat beef, and many eat no meat at all. Muslims do not eat pork. In the north of the country, the staple diet is based on meat, vegetables, and bread such as *chapatis* and *rotis*. In the south, rice plays a much larger part in people's diets, and fish is important in coastal areas. Another staple is *dhal*, a thick stew made from lentils. A common feature of much Indian food is the use of a wide variety of spices, such as cardamom, ginger, saffron, turmeric or coriander, to give endless subtle variations of

◄ These women are making *chapatis* on a simple, wood-burning stove. The *chapati* is a staple part of the diet of northern India.

flavor. Hot green and red chilies are also used in much Indian cooking, giving it a distinctive tongue-stinging intensity.

FAMILY LIFE

Unity of the family group is emphasized heavily in India, and the extended family is still strong. Boys will often follow their fathers into the same job or business. In the north and central parts, and particularly in rural areas, women are still restricted in terms of the work they do and the education they may receive. In some traditional Hindu and Muslim families, women wear a veil and are kept in seclusion from society—although this is now more rare. Nevertheless, it is still very common for a bride to be chosen for a young man by his parents, who may advertise for a suitable partner. Once a girl is married, she moves away from home to join her husband's family. These traditional ways of life are changing, particularly in urban areas, as increasing numbers of women live more independent lives outside the home.

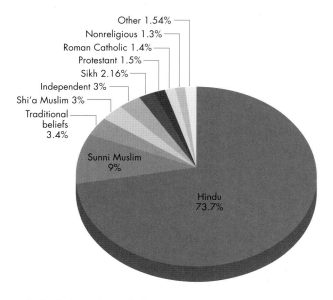

Other 1.54%
Nonreligious 1.3%
Roman Catholic 1.4%
Protestant 1.5%
Sikh 2.16%
Independent 3%
Shi'a Muslim 3%
Traditional beliefs 3.4%
Sunni Muslim 9%
Hindu 73.7%

▲ India's major religions

▲ Visiting the seventh century shrine Pancha Rathas, in Mamallapuram, southern India, this woman is wearing a traditional sari, which is one long piece of fabric wrapped around the waist to form a skirt and then draped, front and back, to cover the blouse.

THE CASTE SYSTEM

The structure of Hindu society is based on an ancient system that originated in one of the Hindu holy books, the *Rig Veda*. According to this scripture, human society is divided into four social classes, or *varnas*: the Brahmins (priests and teachers), Kshatriyas (soldiers and administrators), Vaishyas (merchants and business people) and Shudras (farmers and peasants). All those people who fall outside these classes became known as Untouchables, or later, *Dalits*. They were given tasks that were considered dirty or demeaning, such as cleaning homes, or burying the dead.

This structure of *varnas* later became known as the caste system. In this system, a Hindu is born into a particular *varna* that he or she cannot leave. Although the caste system no longer dictates the type of work a person should follow, it is still a powerful force in Indian society. For example, people from the same caste tend to marry each other. Now, however, any form of discrimination based on caste is illegal, and in the cities, the caste system is becoming less important as other factors, such as education and profession, carry more weight than caste in modern Indian society.

RELIGIONS

Although India is officially a secular country, religion is a central aspect of life for most Indians. Following Partition, Hinduism became the majority faith in India. Today, Hindus make up about 80 percent of the Indian population. Hinduism is unlike most other religions in that it has no founder, no single, central scripture, and no commonly agreed-upon set of teachings. While most Hindus believe in one Supreme God, they worship this One in the form of many deities, and most homes have a room with a small shrine where family members may pray. Hindus worship at dawn and dusk, usually at their home shrines, often by lighting lamps or offering food. Chanting, meditation, and *seva*, service to others and God, are part of a Hindu's religious practices.

Although only just over 12 percent of Indians are Muslims, because of its huge population, India has the third largest Muslim population in the world after Indonesia and Pakistan. In many Indian villages, Hindu temples and Muslim mosques stand side by side.

◀ Indian Muslims offer prayers at the Moti mosque in Bhopal. They are celebrating Eid al-Adha which marks the end of the *hajj* (pilgrimage) to Mecca.

Buddhism, Sikhism, Christianity, and Jainism are the other main religions in India. Buddhism was once widespread in India, but today it is largely confined to the northeast of the country. Sikhism was founded by Guru Nanak in the Punjab in the late sixteenth century. It combines elements of both Hinduism and Islam. The largest concentration of Sikhs live in India's northwest. Jainism has strong links to both Hinduism and Buddhism, and its present-day form originated in the 500s B.C., when a prince called Mahariva taught his followers to consider all living things sacred and to strive for pure lives. Today, India's population of Jains live mostly in the northwest state of Gujurat. Christianity was brought to India in the early centuries of its history, and also by missionaries during the colonial period. A large Christian community lives in the state of Kerala.

▲ These prayer flags are written in the Devanagari script used for Sanskrit and Hindi.

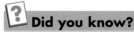 **Did you know?**

Mahatma Gandhi championed the cause of the Untouchables and fought to end discrimination against them. He called them Harijans—"people of God."

Focus on: Hindu Festivals

India has many religious festivals celebrated at different times and by different parts of the community across the country. The main Hindu festivals include *Diwali* and *Holi*. *Diwali* is the festival of lights and, for many Hindus, marks the New Year. It lasts for five days in October or November and is celebrated with the lighting of lamps and candles, musical chants and prayers, and with fireworks. *Holi* marks the beginning of spring and is marked with bonfires and processions of music and dancing, during which people playfully throw colored powders and water at each other.

▲ Indian women throw colored powder and water during Holi celebrations in Kolkata.

 Did you know?

Hindus believe that bathing at Cape Comorin, where the waters of the Indian Ocean, the Arabian Sea, and the Bay of Bengal meet, will wash away their sins. Cleanliness and purity are important aspects of the Hindu religion.

CHAPTER 12

Leisure and Tourism

In India, the dividing line between work and leisure often is not as clear-cut as it is in Western countries, where people typically work from nine to five during the week and relax at the weekends. In many rural areas, "leisure" may not amount to much more than chatting to someone in the market or taking a break from working in the fields. In India's towns and cities, however, many people's increase in material wealth and television exposure to a wider range of leisure activities and sports have brought about many changes.

WATCHING TELEVISION

Television itself represents the biggest change in the way in which people spend their time outside work. The national network, Doordarshan, is controlled by the government and before the 1990s, provided the only TV channels available for Indian viewers. Then, in the early 1990s, international satellite television and cable were introduced and quickly revolutionized the variety of programs on Indian television. Those with access to cable television are now able to watch foreign channels such as the BBC, CNN news, and StarTV, while many Indian satellite companies offer a wide variety of programs, including games shows and soap operas.

? Did you know?

The Indian version of *Who Wants to be a Millionaire?* is the most popular program on Indian TV. In India, it is known as *Kaun Banega Crorepati,* which means literally "Who will become a multi-millionaire?"

◄ Dramatic make-up and hand gestures are the hallmark of Kathakali dancing, a theatrical art form from Kerala in southern India. The popularity of such traditional art forms are threatened by the increased dominance of television in India.

▲ Posters pasted along a street wall advertise the latest Bollywood films.

Focus on: Bollywood

India's film industry is the largest in the world, and Indian films are popular not only at home but also across the world. The industry is known as 'Bollywood'—a combination of Hollywood and Bombay (now known as Mumbai) where most of the films are produced. In 2002, more than 1,200 films were released in India. Bollywood films are often romantic, colorful, "feel-good" musicals or action-packed adventure films and usually have singing and dancing. India's most popular actor, Shashi Kapoor, has starred in countless movies.

PLAYING SPORT

Cricket and soccer have been popular in India since they were imported by the British during colonial times. In fact, Indians are passionate about cricket. During an important match, many people follow the progress of every ball by listening to play-by-play radio descriptions. A match against India's main rival, Pakistan, arouses particular passion and on occasions has led to violent clashes between supporters of the two teams. At times when the two countries suffered great tension over Kashmir, matches between these rivals have been suspended.

Although not as popular as cricket, field hockey is India's national sport. India dominated the world of hockey in the early days of the

▲ Cricket is the sport of choice in India and is played wherever there is enough open space. Supporting the national team is almost like a religion and can bring cities to a halt.

Olympics, winning all six gold medals between 1928 and 1956. Some traditional games are still hugely popular in India, particularly *kabadi*, a game of tag played between two teams. In 2010, India will host the Commonwealth Games in Delhi, and the country is also putting in a bid to host the Summer Olympics in 2016.

TOURISM

India boasts some of the most famous attractions in the world, including the Taj Mahal. In 2002, 2.38 million tourists came to India, 14 percent of whom were from the UK and 10 percent from the United States. Over four million Indians take holidays abroad, but

increasingly, Indians are traveling as tourists in their own country. In 1991, 1.9 million domestic tourists explored India, but this figure rose to 4.9 million by 2002. The potential of the domestic tourist market is only just being realized, and developments such as cheap internal flights are helping to boost this important sector of the economy.

Tourism in India

- Tourist arrivals, millions: 2.384
- Earnings from tourism in U.S.$: 3,041,999,872
- Tourism as % foreign earnings: 5%
- Tourist departures, millions: 4.205

Source: World Bank

India offers the tourist a very wide range of destinations. The beaches of Kerala and Goa have been popular for some time for a relaxing vacation in the sun. Some tourists visit wildlife parks, hoping to see endangered animals such as tigers and lions, while others take tours of India's extraordinary historic buildings, hill forts, temples, and shrines. Eco-tourism, which provides tours that make as little impact as possible on the local ecology while benefiting the lives of local people, is also becoming increasingly popular in India, with vacations such as bird-watching and safaris.

Another form of vacation that has become increasingly popular is the "yoga vacation." *Hatha yoga* is a form of physical and mental exercise that has its roots in Hinduism. It is practiced widely in the West, and many people come to India to stay in an *ashram*—a religious community—and learn *hatha yoga* in the country in which it originated. Yoga means "union" in Sanskrit. Many other forms of yoga are part of the Hindu tradition, including meditation and breathing practices that are designed to help a practitioner attain union with God.

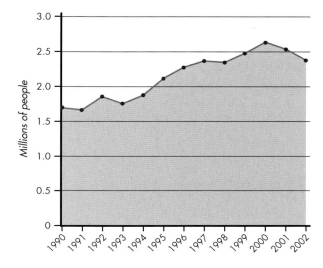

▲ Changes in international tourism, 1990–2002

Focus on: The "Golden Triangle"

The most popular tourist circuit in India explores three cities in the north of the country—India's capital, Delhi; the Mogul city of Agra; and Jaipur, the capital of the state of Rajasthan. The tour, known as the "Golden Triangle," can be covered in a week and also includes India's most-visited site, the Taj Mahal. The Indian government is also interested in promoting the country's many other lesser-known attractions, for example, the fabulous temples of southern India and the exotic delights of the Thar Desert. Adventure vacations, including Himalayan mountaineering, white-water rafting, and hiking, are also marketed for overseas and domestic tourists.

▲ The Taj Mahal in Agra was built by the Mogul emperor Shah Jahan as a tomb for his favorite wife.

CHAPTER 13

Environment and Conservation

Ind ndia has an extraordinary variety of landscapes, plants, and animals, including Indian elephants and some of the world's most endangered species, such as the Bengal tiger and the Ganges river dolphin. The country's expanding population and its headlong dash to industrialize, however, have put ever-increasing pressure on its delicate ecosystems.

ENVIRONMENT AND THE GOVERNMENT

In 1984, a gas leak at the partly U.S.-owned Union Carbide chemical plant in Bhopal, in central India, killed more than 3,000 people. Thousands more were seriously injured by the poisonous gas. This incident raised awareness of environmental and safety issues in industry, and

Focus on: Project Tiger

About 1900, an estimated 40,000 tigers lived in India, but by 1972, there were only 1,827 left. A national ban on tiger hunting was imposed, and Project Tiger was set up. By 2002, the tiger population stood at 3,642. Now, twenty-seven Project Tiger reserves cover nearly 14,700 sq miles (38,000 sq km) of India. Nonetheless, India's tigers are still threatened by poachers and other people, such as miners, who want to use the

reserved land. Problems also arise with local communities who live near or on the edges of reserves, and who see the tigers as a threat to both themselves and their livelihoods. The future survival of the tigers can be helped if local people are consulted more carefully about decisions that affect them, and if those who have to coexist with the tigers receive benefits from tiger conservation, such as income from tourism.

◀ Two Bengal tigers take a swim in one of India's national parks. The tiger is a protected animal in India.

led to the creation of a new department in the Indian government, the Ministry of Environment and Forests (MoEF). The MoEF took charge of all areas of conservation and protection of wildlife and the environment, as well as pollution-monitoring and control. Nevertheless, policies to promote the country's economy have usually won out over India's environmental policies, and, as a result, India faces some major environmental problems.

AIR POLLUTION

Together with water pollution, air pollution is one of the most serious environmental problems in India, causing thousands of deaths every year. Urban areas such as Delhi, Mumbai, and Kolkata are some of the most polluted cities in the world. Their pollution is the result of increased traffic emissions as well as industrial activity. Measures to curb this pollution have been introduced but are often not effectively enforced. Diesel-powered vehicles, which cause high levels of air pollution, are now banned from the center of Delhi and all buses are now

being converted from diesel to compressed natural gas. In Bangalore, motorists turn off their engines while waiting at traffic lights to reduce pollution.

India's rapid industrialization has also had a major impact on its carbon dioxide (CO_2)

▲ A motorcyclist, wearing a traditional turban, also wears a scarf to protect himself from traffic fumes near the Chandi Chowk bazaar in Delhi.

Environmental and conservation data

📂 Forested area as % total land area: 8%
📂 Protected area as % total land area: 5.2%
📂 Number of protected areas: 545

SPECIES DIVERSITY

Category	Known species	Threatened species
Mammals	390	88
Breeding birds	458	72
Reptiles	521	25
Amphibians	231	3
Fish	5,749	9
Plants	18,664	244

Source: World Resources Institute

emissions. CO_2 is given off when fossil fuels such as oil, coal, and natural gas are burned, and is a major factor in global warming. In 2002, India had the fifth highest levels of CO_2 emissions in the world, with 4.2 percent of the global total. This amount is still low compared to the United States (23.4 percent) or China (13.6 percent). Because they are the world's most rapidly expanding economies, however, growth in emissions from both China and India is expected to outstrip that of other countries soon. Bringing India's CO_2 emissions under control, while continuing to allow the country to develop economically, is vital as part of the international strategy to tackle the problem of global warming.

FARMING ACTIVITIES

The activities of farmers are often at odds with conservation and protection of the environment. Modern farming methods use artificial fertilizers and pesticides, which often contain harmful chemicals that pollute groundwater supplies. Although national parks and wildlife sanctuaries have been designated, farmers often illegally use this land for cultivation. Elephants are still illegally killed for ivory from their tusks, in spite of the world ivory trade ban by the Convention on International Trade in Endangered Species, which has been in effect since the early 1990s.

DEFORESTATION

Deforestation is another major environmental issue in India. Chopping down trees for both industrial and agricultural use has left soils bare and resulted in severe soil erosion. Without tree roots to anchor the soil, many dams are beginning to silt up, as unprotected soil runs off the surrounding hillsides into reservoirs. Trees absorb CO_2 and give off oxygen, so the removal of tree cover has also affected the levels of CO_2 in the atmosphere.

WATER RESOURCES

Despite the annual monsoon rains and the floods that they often bring, clean water for drinking is a scarce resource in India. Population growth and rapid urbanization have put great pressure on the water supply, and many people in India have to line up every day at communal water taps to pick up their supplies of water. Water is needed for industry and to irrigate land for crop production, but a rapid and unregulated increase in demand in some places has depleted groundwater reserves to dangerous levels, drying up rivers and making soils dry and prone to erosion.

▲ These trees were felled on the Western Ghats to provide fuel for nearby tea-processing factories.

In the past, most villagers got their water from hand-operated wells, limiting the amount of water they could draw in a day and the depth of the well. The introduction of pump-operated wells has allowed water to be obtained more easily, and from deeper wells, often sucking underground reserves dry. In urban areas, such as Bangalore, an estimated 40 percent of water is wasted in transportation. While the construction of big dams to create reservoirs to store water has been one solution supported by the government in the past, because of the environmental and social problems connected with big dam projects, many people now favor smaller, local projects to address the water crisis. The Integrated Watershed Development Program is funded by the government and allows communities to construct small

dams and other structures to store rainwater and replenish groundwater supplies. The "integrated" approach of this program also aims to address other environmental problems, such as deforestation and soil erosion, that relate to water conservation.

▲ Young children pump water from a well in Uttar Pradesh.

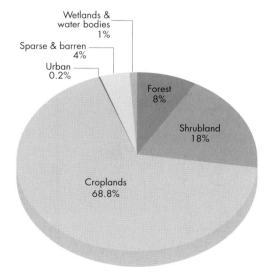

▲ Types of habitat

Wetlands & water bodies 1%
Sparse & barren 4%
Urban 0.2%
Forest 8%
Shrubland 18%
Croplands 68.8%

Focus on: Scrapping ships

Half the world's ocean-going fleet ends its life on a beach at Alang, in Gujarat state. Here, ships are dismantled and the pieces sold off as scrap. Many of the ships that arrive in Alang could not be broken up in their home countries because of strict environmental laws. The ships are often full of pollutants, such as asbestos, heavy metals and toxic paints, and the local environment is suffering as a result.

CHAPTER 14

Future Challenges

I ndia is a country in the process of very rapid economic and social development. Any country undergoing such changes has to come to terms with their impact, and India is no exception. Traditional customs are being challenged, especially in urban areas where satellite TV, tourism, foreign businesses, and shops have brought new ideas and ways of life, particularly for young people.

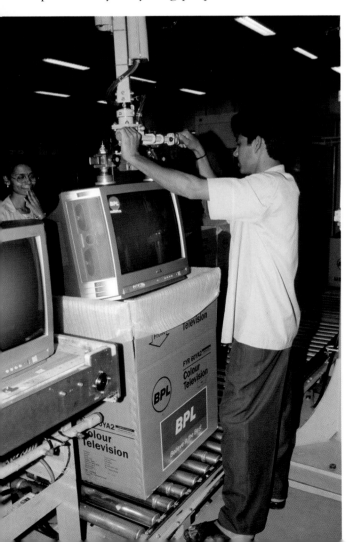

◀ Television sets are packaged for export in Agra.

INDIA'S POPULATION

One of the most pressing problems for the future is India's population growth. The expanding population has already put huge pressure on India's environment, on agriculture, and on the country's infrastructure—its roads, railways, education, and health care. Although many Indians have benefited from the country's breath-taking economic growth since the early 1990s, many millions of people, mainly in rural areas, still live in poverty and struggle with disease and malnutrition. Providing adequate food, health care, and education for all, and therefore bridging the gap between the wealthy and the poor, is one of the main challenges for the Indian government for the future.

KEEPING THE PEACE

India's relations with its neighbor Pakistan present another major challenge, particularly as both countries have nuclear weapons. Recent developments have been hopeful: A meeting between the Indian prime minister Manmohan Singh and the Pakistani president Pervez Musharraf in April 2005 ended in a joint statement from the two leaders stating that peace between the two countries was now "irreversible." Although the dispute over Kashmir has yet to be finally resolved, the need for the two countries to work together in the region was starkly highlighted by the aftermath of the earthquake in October 2005 which killed more than 75,000 people and left about 3.5

million homeless. India will also have to keep peace between its Hindu and Muslim populations. Although the BJP is no longer in power, the Hindu majority has a powerful voice in the country. The balance between different communities needs to be carefully maintained.

▲ A group of young children play and wash in the slum district of Mumbai. Hundreds of thousands of children live in these conditions all over the city, and improving the quality of their life is one of the major challenges for India in the future.

LOOK TO THE FUTURE

Many times in its past, India has accommodated and absorbed different cultures, and the country prides itself on its ability to assimilate diverse people into its complex, multiethnic society. Despite the problems it faces, India has many reasons to be optimistic about its own future. The key to India's future development lies in the strength of its people and its

economy. Many Indians who would once have emigrated to countries such as the United States are now choosing to stay at home to work in India's thriving economy. Although India suffers from low levels of literacy among the poor, it nevertheless has an excellent university system that produces the well-trained graduates who have helped to fuel its economic growth. India is a fast-developing country that now becoming a major player on the world stage.

Time Line

c. 3500 B.C. Settlement starts in the fertile valley of the Indus River.

c. 2500 B.C. Indus Valley civilization reaches its peak.

c. 1700 B.C. Indus Valley civilization declines.

c. 1500 B.C. Aryans from central Asia begin to move south into India.

c. 1500-1200 B.C. Hindu *Vedas* written.

c. 500 B.C. Buddhism is founded in India.

530 B.C. Persians invade India.

326 B.C. Greeks, led by Alexander the Great, invade India.

321-184 B.C. Mauryan Empire rules India.

272-232 B.C. Mauryan emperor, Asoka, reigns over India.

320 B.C.– 500 A.D. Gupta Empire rules India

700s Muslims reach India.

1192 Muslim armies conquer much of northern India and establish Delhi Sultanate (1206).

1398 Mongol leader Timur sacks Delhi.

1498 Portuguese sailor Vasco da Gama lands at Calicut in India.

c. 1500 Guru Nanak founds the Sikh religion.

1526 Babur founds the Mogul Empire.

1857 Indians stage uprising against British rule.

1858 End of Mogul Empire. British government takes over rule of India from the East India Company.

1885 Indian National Congress Party founded.

1914-1918 Indian troops fight on the side of the British in World War I.

1919 British massacre more than four hundred in Amritsar.

1920 Mahatma Gandhi starts civil disobedience campaign against the British.

1930 Mahatma Gandhi leads the Salt March.

1947 (15 August) India becomes independent. Jawaharlal Nehru is India's first prime minister. Thousands of people die after Partition of India from Pakistan.

1948 Mahatma Gandhi assassinated. War with Pakistan over Kashmir.

1965 Second war with Pakistan over Kashmir.

1966 Indira Gandhi becomes prime minister.

1971 War with Pakistan; East Pakistan becomes Bangladesh.

1975 Indira Gandhi declares state of emergency (until 1977).

1984 Indian troops storm Sikh Golden Temple at Amritsar. Indira Gandhi assassinated. Bhopal gas leak kills more than 3,000 people.

1991 Rajiv Ganghi assassinated.

1992 Demolition of Babri mosque at Ayodhya leads to widespread violence between Hindus and Muslims.

2001 Earthquake in Gujarat kills at least 30,000 people.

2002 More than eight hundred people die in violence between Hindus and Muslims.

2003 cease-fire agreed in Kashmir.

2004 India starts to withdraw troops from Kashmir. Manmohan Singh becomes first Sikh to be India's prime minister. A huge tsunami kills thousands on India's east coast.

2005 Floods and landslides kill more than 1,000 people in Mumbai and the Maharashtra region. An earthquake kills 75,000 in Kashmir, leaving more than 3.5 million homeless.

Glossary

alluvial describes clay and silt deposited by slow-moving rivers. Alluvial soils are usually very fertile

Aryans people originally from central Asia who moved south into India around 1500 B.C.

biotechnology the study and use of living microorganisms in industrial processes

Buddhism a world religion that started about 2,500 years ago. The founder of Buddhism was Siddhartha Gautama (c. 563–483 B.C.), who became known as the Buddha—the "enlightened one."

cash crops crops that are grown to be sold for profit

caste system in Indian Hindu society, the system by which a person's place in society is determined at birth

colony a territory that is ruled by another country

compensation money paid as reparation for loss or injury

constitution an agreed set of rules and laws

deforestation the clearance of trees from land that was once covered by forest

deity a god or goddess

democracy a political system in which representatives are chosen by the people in free elections

dowry money or property brought by a woman to a marriage, or money paid by the groom to a bride or her parents

Dravidians the native people of India before the arrival of the Aryans

dynasty a series of rulers from the same family who succeed one another in power

ecosystems systems made up of relationships between living things and their surrounding environments

ethnic a way of grouping people according to shared customs, beliefs, and often language.

federal a way of organizing a country so that governing power is shared between the central government and regional governments

fossil fuels types of energy sources, such as oil, coal, and gas, that are formed by fossilized plants and animals. They release carbon dioxide when they are burned.

genetically modified plants or other organisms in which the genes have been deliberately altered or moved in order to improve the organism in some way

Hindi the official language of India (along with English); one of the family of Indo-European languages

Hindu Describes a follower of Hinduism, the religion of the majority of Indians. Hindus worship god in the form of many gods and goddesses and believe that a person is reborn many times into many different lives.

hybrid an animal or plant that is the result of cross-breeding between different species

hydroelectric power the production of electricity by harnessing the power of moving water

industrialization the process of developing factories and manufacturing on a large scale

malnutrition deficiency in the nutrients that are essential for the development and maintenance of the body

monsoon the seasonal winds that are generated by the difference in air temperatures over the Asian landmass and the sea, which bring regular rainfall to the Indian subcontinent

mosque a Muslim place of worship

Muslim a follower of the religion of Islam, which states that there is only one God, and Muhammad is his prophet

nationalist a person or movement with a strong commitment to the culture and interests of their own country

Partition the term given to the division of India along religious lines into India and Pakistan at Independence

republic a country that has a president rather than a king or queen as its head of state

Sanskrit the ancient language of India, the language in which the Hindu sacred texts, the *Vedas*, were written

secular non-religious; not supporting any one religion

Sikh a follower of the monotheistic religion founded by Guru Nanak in the Punjab in the late sixteenth century that rejects both Hindu and Muslim forms of worship

socialist a supporter of socialism, an economic system in which means of production, such as land and factories, are owned by the state, rather than by private individuals

subcontinent A large landmass that forms a separate, distinct part of a continent

subsidies Money paid by a government or other body to help a particular group of people

subsistence farming Farming where crops provide only enough food for the farming family

tariffs taxes on imports, often used to keep foreign goods from being cheaper than domestic products

tsunami a giant wave caused by an undersea earthquake

urbanization the movement of people from rural areas to towns and cities

Further Information

BOOKS TO READ

Bowden, Rob.
A River Journey: The Ganges.
Hodder Wayland, 2003.

Chatterjee Manini, and Anita Roy.
India. Eyewitness Guides (series).
Dorling Kindersley, 2002.

Cumming David.
The Changing Face of India.
Hodder Wayland, 2001.

Dalal, Anita.
Nations of the World: India
Raintree, 2001.

Demi.
Gandhi.
Margaret K. McElderry, 2001.

Das, Rasamandala.
Hinduism. Religions of the World (series).
World Almanac Library, 2006.

Ganeri, Anita.
Buddhism.
Religions of the World (series).
World Almanac Library, 2006.

Rowe, Percy, and Patience Coster.
Delhi.
Cities of the World (series).
World Almanac Library, 2005.

Self, David.
Islam.
Religions of the World (series).
World Almanac Library, 2006.

USEFUL WEB SITES

BBC country profile and links to latest news from India
news.bbc.co.uk/1/hi/world/south_asia/country_profiles/1154019.stm

CIA World Factbook facts and figures for India
www.cia.gov/library/publications/the-world-factbook/index.html

Directory of Indian government Web sites
goidirectory.nic.in/

Education for underprivileged children in India
www.ashanet.org/info.html

Government of India
indiaimage.nic.in/

Project Tiger
projecttiger.nic.in/

Index

Page numbers in **bold**
indicate pictures.

About the Authors

Ali Brownlie Bojang is a former teacher of humanities and an education officer for Oxfam. She has written a number of books for young people as well as course materials for teachers.

Nicola Barber is the author of many nonfiction children's books, specializing in geography, history and the arts.